It's My State!

VIRGINIA

The Old Dominion State

Laura L. Sullivan, David C. King II, Stephanie Fitzgerald

Cavendish Square
New York

Published in 2015 by Cavendish Square Publishing, LLC
243 5th Avenue, Suite 136, New York, NY 10016

First Edition

Website: cavendishsq.com

This publication represents the opinions and views of the author based on his or her personal experience, knowledge, and research. The information in this book serves as a general guide only. The author and publisher have used their best efforts in preparing this book and disclaim liability rising directly or indirectly from the use and application of this book.

CPSIA Compliance Information: Batch #WW15CSQ

All websites were available and accurate when this book was sent to press.

Library of Congress Cataloging-in-Publication Data

Sullivan, Laura L.
Virginia / Laura L. Sullivan, David C. King II, Stephanie Fitzgerald. — Third edition.
pages cm. — (It's my state!)
Includes index.
ISBN 978-1-50260-019-6 (hardcover) ISBN 978-1-50260-020-2 (ebook)
1. Virginia—History. I. Virginia. II. Title.

F94.3.B87 2015
974.6—dc23

2014020999

Editor: Fletcher Doyle
Senior Copy Editor: Wendy A. Reynolds
Art Director: Jeffrey Talbot
Designer: Joseph Macri
Senior Production Manager: Jennifer Ryder-Talbot
Production Editor: David McNamara
Photo Research by J8 Media

Printed in the United States of America

VIRGINIA
CONTENTS

★ State Tree and Flower: American Dogwood

Also called the flowering dogwood, this tree is best known for its beautiful blossoms—white or pink with small yellow centers—that are a sure sign of spring. Dogwoods grow throughout Virginia in the wild as well as in neighborhood gardens and yards.

★ State Bird: Northern Cardinal

This bright red songbird is known for the pointed crest on its head and for its deep red feathers. Females, which are less brilliantly colored than males, are usually dull reddish brown. The cardinal's song is a clear, piercing whistle.

★ State Dog: American Foxhound

This hunting dog can trace its roots to colonial times. The English brought hounds with them to America in the 1600s, the descendants of which were bred with French hounds that had been given to George Washington, resulting in the American foxhound.

VIRGINIA ★ ★ ★ ★ ★
POPULATION: 8,001,024

★ **State Shell: Virginia Oyster**

The Virginia oyster was a crucial food source for the Native Americans who first inhabited the area. Today, it is one of the most valuable shellfish for North American fishers.

★ **State Insect: Tiger Swallowtail Butterfly**

Known for the bright yellow and black stripes on their body and wings, Tiger Swallowtails are one of the most common butterflies in the eastern United States. The largest species can have a wingspan of more than 6 inches (15 centimeters).

★ **State Beverage: Milk**

In 1982, milk became Virginia's official beverage. Almost a hundred thousand dairy cows are located on farms across the state—the greatest numbers are in Rockingham County. These cows produce almost two billion pounds (900 million kilograms) of milk in a single year.

Virginia Beach has one of the longest stretches of pleasure beach in the world, as well as 35 miles (56 km) of waterfront property.

The Old Dominion State

Virginia has 39,594 square miles (102,548 square kilometers) of land area. It is the thirty-seventh largest state. It is made up of ninety-five counties, plus thirty-nine independent cities. Richmond is the state capital, but Virginia Beach is the city with the biggest population.

The state includes a remarkable variety of landforms for its size. The coastal region includes marshy lowlands, beautiful sand beaches, and a large swamp area. Moving inland, the lowlands change into the rolling hills of the Piedmont. Still farther west are two mountain ranges with dramatic views and hundreds of miles of hiking trails. Nestled between the Blue Ridge Mountains and the Allegheny Mountains is the scenic and **fertile** Shenandoah Valley, one of America's great natural treasures.

Virginia's Eastern Shore

The geography of eastern Virginia is dominated by Chesapeake **Bay**—a huge arm of the Atlantic Ocean. The bay reaches more than 200 miles (320 km) inland. The long, narrow strip of land that forms the eastern boundary of the bay is called the Delmarva Peninsula. The word *Delmarva* was created out of the names of the three states that occupy the strip of land—Delaware, Maryland, and Virginia. Some Virginians call the region the Eastern

The Chesapeake Bay Bridge Tunnel connected Virginia Beach to the Delmarva Peninsula in 1964.

Shore. Until bridges were built connecting the Eastern Shore to the mainland in 1964, residents there and on the nearby islands were quite isolated.

Offshore, or barrier, islands give this sliver of land some protection from Atlantic storms. They include Assateague and Chincoteague islands, which are famous for their semiwild Chincoteague ponies.

Chesapeake Bay

Chesapeake Bay is a unique body of water. It is America's largest **estuary**—a partially enclosed area where fresh river waters and salty ocean waters meet. More than 150 of Virginia's major rivers and streams empty into the Chesapeake, including the Potomac, Rappahannock, York, and James rivers. A broad inlet connects Chesapeake Bay with the James River to form Hampton Roads, one of the world's largest natural harbors. In 1862, during the Civil War, Hampton Roads was the scene of the world's first clash between two ironclad warships. The USS *Monitor* faced off against the CSS *Virginia* (often called the *Merrimack*—its name while part of the U.S. fleet) in an effort to protect the USS *Minnesota*. Neither side won the battle, but the *Minnesota* remained unharmed. Both the *Monitor* and the *Virginia* survived the battle without much damage—and ushered in a new era of shipbuilding.

The warm, shallow waters of the bay are filled with schools of fish and large colonies of shellfish—oysters, clams, and the famous Chesapeake blue crabs. On most days of the year, this inland sea swarms with sailboats, speedboats, and fishing vessels.

The Tidewater Region

Virginia's section of the Atlantic Coast region, a belt of lowland called the Coastal Plain that stretches from New York to Florida, is known as the Tidewater because ocean tides reach all the way into Chesapeake Bay and Virginia's four main rivers. From north to south, Virginia's coast measures about 112 miles (180 km), but all the inlets and bays, plus the Eastern Shore, create a coastline of more than 3,000 miles (almost 5,000 km).

The state's largest urban area is on the southern part of the Tidewater, including the port cities of Newport News and Norfolk, as well as Virginia Beach. Virginia Beach has about 35 miles (56 km) of beautiful white sand beach lined with modern high-rise apartment buildings. Huge ports are located in Newport News and Norfolk, which is also home to the world's largest naval station.

South of the James River is an enormous wetland named the Great Dismal Swamp. This protected area is nearly 600 square miles (1,500 sq. km) and extends into North Carolina.

The battleship USS *Wisconsin* is berthed near the National Maritime Center in Norfolk.

VIRGINIA
COUNTY MAP

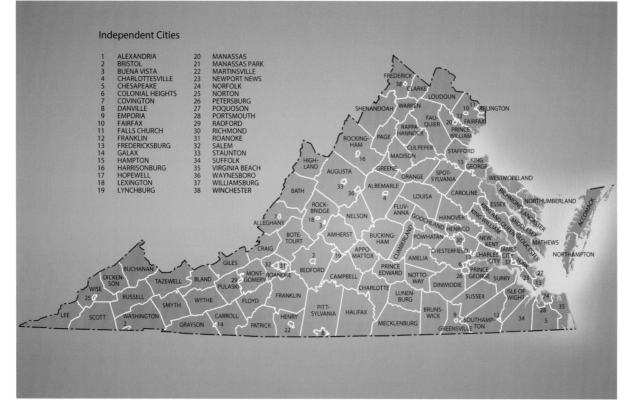

Independent Cities

1	ALEXANDRIA	20	MANASSAS
2	BRISTOL	21	MANASSAS PARK
3	BUENA VISTA	22	MARTINSVILLE
4	CHARLOTTESVILLE	23	NEWPORT NEWS
5	CHESAPEAKE	24	NORFOLK
6	COLONIAL HEIGHTS	25	NORTON
7	COVINGTON	26	PETERSBURG
8	DANVILLE	27	POQUOSON
9	EMPORIA	28	PORTSMOUTH
10	FAIRFAX	29	RADFORD
11	FALLS CHURCH	30	RICHMOND
12	FRANKLIN	31	ROANOKE
13	FREDERICKSBURG	32	SALEM
14	GALAX	33	STAUNTON
15	HAMPTON	34	SUFFOLK
16	HARRISONBURG	35	VIRGINIA BEACH
17	HOPEWELL	36	WAYNESBORO
18	LEXINGTON	37	WILLIAMSBURG
19	LYNCHBURG	38	WINCHESTER

Accomack	33,164	Brunswick	17,434	Covington*	5,961
Albemarle	98,970	Buchanan	24,098	Craig	5,190
Alexandria*	139,966	Buckingham	17,146	Culpeper	46,689
Alleghany	16,250	Buena Vista*	6,650	Cumberland	10,052
Amelia	12,690	Campbell	54,842	Danville*	43,055
Amherst	32,353	Caroline	28,545	Dickenson	15,903
Appomattox	14,973	Carroll	30,042	Dinwiddie	28,001
Arlington	207,627	Charles City	7,256	Emporia*	5,927
Augusta	73,750	Charlotte	12,586	Essex	11,151
Bath	4,731	Charlottesville*	43,475	Fairfax	1,081,726
Bedford	68,676	Chesapeake*	222,209	Fairfax City*	22,565
Bland	6,824	Chesterfield	316,326	Falls Church*	12,332
Botetourt	33,148	Clarke	14,034	Fauquier	65,203
Bristol*	17,835	Colonial Heights*	17,411	Floyd	15,279

VIRGINIA ★ ★ ★ ★
POPULATION BY COUNTY AND CITY

Fluvanna	25,691	Martinsville*	13,821	Scott	23,177
Franklin	56,259	Mathews	8,978	Shenandoah	41,993
Franklin City*	8,582	Mecklenburg	32,727	Smyth	32,208
Frederick	78,305	Middlesex	10,959	Southampton	18,570
Fredericksburg*	24,286	Montgomery	94,392	Spotsylvania	122,397
Galax*	7,042	Nelson	15,020	Stafford	128,961
Giles	17,286	New Kent	18,429	Staunton*	23,746
Gloucester	36,858	Newport News*	180,719	Suffolk*	84,585
Goochland	24,717	Norfolk*	242,803	Surry	7,058
Grayson	15,533	Northampton	12,389	Sussex	12,087
Greene	18,403	Northumberland	12,330	Tazewell	45,078
Greensville	12,243	Norton*	3,958	Virginia Beach*	437,994
Halifax	36,241	Nottoway	15,853	Warren	37,575
Hampton*	137,436	Orange	33,481	Washington	54,876
Hanover	99,863	Page	24,042	Waynesboro*	21,006
Harrisonburg*	48,914	Patrick	18,490	Westmoreland	17,454
Henrico	306,935	Petersburg*	32,420	Williamsburg*	14,068
Henry	54,151	Pittsylvania	63,506	Winchester*	26,203
Highland	2,321	Poquoson*	12,150	Wise	41,452
Hopewell*	22,591	Portsmouth*	95,535	Wythe	29,235
Isle of Wight	35,270	Powhatan	28,046	York	65,464
James City	67,009	Prince Edward	23,368		
King and Queen	6,945	Prince George	35,725		
King George	23,584	Prince William	402,002		
King William	15,935	Pulaski	34,872		
Lancaster	11,391	Radford*	16,408		
Lee	25,587	Rappahannock	7,373		
Lexington*	7,042	Richmond	9,254		
Loudoun	312,311	Richmond City*	204,214		
Louisa	33,153	Roanoke	92,376		
Lunenburg	12,914	Roanoke City*	97,032		
Lynchburg*	75,568	Rockbridge	22,307		
Madison	13,308	Rockingham	76,314		
Manassas*	37,821	Russell	28,897		
Manassas Park*	14,273	Salem*	24,802		

* Marks one of Virginia's thirty-eight independent cities, which are separate from any county. There are only three other independent cities in the U.S.: Baltimore, Maryland; St. Louis, Missouri; and Carson City, Nevada.

Source: U.S. Bureau of the Census, 2010

In 1763, George Washington surveyed the swamp and saw its potential for timber production. He formed a company called the Dismal Swamp Land Company to drain and log parts of the swamp. Logging proved very successful and, along with commercial and residential development, destroyed much of the ecosystem. The remaining area, which became the Great Dismal Swamp National Wildlife Refuge in 1974, is less than half the size of the original swamp.

Much of the swamp has been drained. In December 2013, a project was completed to return water to 9,580 acres (3877 hectares) of state and federal land that were drained more than sixty years earlier.

From the mid-1600s through the 1800s, sprawling farms called **plantations** were built on the banks of the Tidewater rivers. Tobacco was the major cash crop of the early plantations, and after 1800, wheat became important.

These plantations, some of which still exist, were like independent villages. Each had its own orchard, vegetable garden, blacksmith shop, and carpenter—as well as a church. Rivers such as the James, York, and Rappahannock served as highways. Sailing ships carried the planters' crops to market towns and brought back merchandise from other East Coast cities and from Europe. Boats navigated the rivers to the Fall Line—the point where the soft Coastal Plain meets the harder rock of the inland hill country.

Virginia Borders

North:	Maryland
	West Virginia
	Washington, DC
South:	North Carolina
	Tennessee
East:	Maryland
	Atlantic Ocean
West:	Kentucky
	West Virginia

The Piedmont

West of the Tidewater is a region called the Piedmont. It covers the central third of the state. The Piedmont features a rolling landscape that is about 50 miles (80 km) wide in the north, broadening to about 100 miles (160 km) wide in the south. The Piedmont stretches from the Blue Ridge Mountains in the west to the Fall Line.

As the Tidewater region filled with settlers in the early 1700s, pioneer families moved into the Piedmont. Most started small farms, but there were also a number of tobacco plantations. Family-owned farms, including apple and peach orchards, still cover the foothills of the Blue Ridge Mountains today. Some of the Piedmont is also now known as "horse country," famous for its traditions of foxhunting and horse breeding.

The Western Mountains

The Blue Ridge Mountains extend from Harper's Ferry, West Virginia, south into Georgia. The mountains form one of America's outstanding scenic areas. Two of the nation's most beautiful roads—Skyline Drive, and the Blue Ridge Parkway—wind along the crest of these mountains and upland meadows. The northern road, Skyline Drive, twists and turns for 105 miles (169 km), with a maximum speed limit of 35 miles per hour (56 kmh). The southern road, the Blue Ridge Parkway, extends another 469 miles (755 km), from Shenandoah National Park in northern Virginia to Great Smoky Mountains National Park in North Carolina.

Virginia Hurricanes

In 1788, a storm known as George Washington's Hurricane hit, causing severe flooding. In 1821, there was a hurricane so strong it created what residents called a tidal wave. More recently, hurricanes to strike Virginia were Isabel in 2003, Gaston in 2004, and Irene in 2011.

Skyline Drive provides beautiful views in the Blue Ridge Mountains.

★ 10 KEY SITES ★ ★ ★

Arlington National Cemetery

1. Arlington National Cemetery

Established during the American Civil War, Arlington National Cemetery is the final resting place of thousands of honored veterans. The Third U.S. Infantry Regiment constantly guards the Tomb of the Unknown Soldier, which commemorates the unidentified soldiers of several wars.

2. Colonial Williamsburg

Colonial Williamsburg recreates an authentic colonial American city. Interpreters dress, work, and speak as they did in the colonial era, showing visitors what life was truly like back then. Its motto is, "That the future may learn from the past."

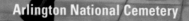

Williamsburg

3. Great Falls Park

Spreading over 800 acres, this national park along the Potomac River has a series of twenty-foot (32 km) falls, as well as hiking trails and cliffs frequented by rock climbers. There is also a visitor center and viewing platforms.

4. Manassas National Battlefield Park

The tranquil Virginia countryside at this location saw two terrible battles during the American Civil War—the First and Second Battles of Bull Run (also called the Battles of Manassas.) Visitors now explore the historic grounds, interpretive programs, and museum.

Manassas National Battlefield

5. Monticello

U.S. President Thomas Jefferson spent most of his time on his plantation, and is buried on the grounds. The neoclassical mansion sits on extensive acreage with lovely gardens. Visitors can learn about President Jefferson, and the history of slavery at Monticello.

VIRGINIA ★ ★ ★ ★ ★

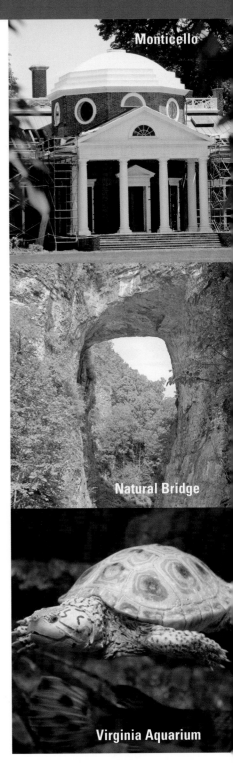

6. Mount Vernon

The first president of the United States, George Washington, made his home at Mount Vernon along the banks of the Potomac River. Today, Mount Vernon hosts tours, reenactments, and festivals. It is Washington's final resting place.

7. The Natural Bridge

Some people consider the Natural Bridge one of the wonders of the world. Formed when a cavern collapsed, leaving the stone bridge intact, the park features hiking trails, caverns to explore, and a living history exhibit of Monacan Indian culture.

8. Skyline Drive

This road along the crest of the Blue Ridge Mountains meanders for 105 miles (169 km) from Front Royal to Interstate 64 near Waynesboro. Seventy-five overlooks provide vistas of the Shenandoah Valley to the west and the piedmont to the east.

9. Virginia Aquarium

The aquarium at Virginia Beach is home to thousands of species of marine life. Guests can get up close and personal with sea animals at the Chesapeake Bay Touch Pool, and learn about the Chesapeake Bay's signature species, the blue crab.

10. Virginia Beach

This resort city has something for everyone, from the boardwalk on Oceanside to restaurants, beaches, museums, and theaters. The area is known for many festivals, including the popular Neptune Festival, a big air show, and the American Music Festival.

Monticello

Natural Bridge

Virginia Aquarium

In general, the Blue Ridge Mountains vary in height from 2,000 to 4,000 feet (600 to 1,200 meters). One exceptionally high point in the range—and the highest point in the state—is Mount Rogers, which is 5,729 feet (1,746 m) above sea level.

The Blue Ridge Mountains and the more rugged Allegheny Mountains to the west are among the oldest mountains in the world. Over thousands of years, the forces of wind and water slowly wore away the jagged peaks to create more gentle landforms. The two scenic roads through the Blue Ridge provide breathtaking views of the Piedmont hills to the east and the Alleghenies to the west. The leaves of the hardwood trees on the slopes of the Blue Ridge—maple, hickory, white oak, and others—turn dazzling colors in the autumn.

The Allegheny Mountains, one of the ranges in the Appalachian chain, are on Virginia's border with Kentucky. For America's pioneers, these mountains formed a more imposing barrier than the Blue Ridge. It was not until 1775 that Daniel Boone led a group

Hikers in Shenandoah National Park cool their feet.

of woodsmen to **blaze** the Wilderness Road trail through a pass called the Cumberland Gap from southwest Virginia into what became Kentucky. Thousands of families followed Boone's road.

The Shenandoah Valley

When the first pioneers entered the Shenandoah Valley around 1700, they saw herds of bison roaming fertile grasslands watered by the Shenandoah River. By the late 1700s, the bison—and most Native American groups—had retreated farther west. Land-hungry settlers poured into the valley and established small family-owned farms, many of which are still in operation today.

The northern end of the valley, which is approximately 150 miles (240 km) long, is anchored by Winchester, the capital of Virginia's well-known apple orchard region. The orchards and wheat fields of the Shenandoah were important to the South during the Civil War. The valley also formed a natural north-south highway for the South's armies.

The Luray Caverns are decorated with hanging stalactites and with stalagmites that rise from the cave floor.

The Blue Ridge Parkway is lined with colors in the autumn.

In June 1863, for example, the famous Confederate general Robert E. Lee led his Army of Northern Virginia north through the valley, using the Blue Ridge Mountains to shield his movements from the North's armies in the east. The next month, after the Confederate defeat at Gettysburg, Pennsylvania, Lee used the valley for his retreat.

Today, the Shenandoah Valley is a popular tourist area. The valley is dotted with Civil War battle sites and historic homes, including the birthplace of President Woodrow Wilson and the headquarters of Civil War general Thomas "Stonewall" Jackson. Visitors are also drawn to such natural wonders as the Natural Bridge and the Luray Caverns.

Climate

The Virginia climate offers something for everyone. Along the coast, people enjoy long summers and mild winters. Farmers like the Tidewater growing season, which lasts up to eight months—three months longer than in the western part of the state. Although the Tidewater receives only a few inches of snow every year, the mountains see up to 23 inches (58 cm).

The overall climate of Virginia is mild. But the ocean affects weather and climate, making summers generally cooler near the coast, and winters less severe. January temperatures close to sea level average about 42 degrees Fahrenheit (6 degrees Celsius), while in the mountains, the average January temperature is about 31°F (–1°C).

Virginia Wildlife

Forests cover about 65 percent of Virginia's land area. Some of the state's most common trees include oaks, pines, maples, hickory, and beech. In the fall many of the leaves turn brilliant shades of orange, red, or yellow. The state has many different types of plants, including ferns and native grasses. In warmer months, wisteria, lilies, azaleas, mountain laurels, and bluebells make colorful floral additions to the state's impressive scenery.

Thanks to its varied landscapes and ecosystems, Virginia is home to an incredible array of wildlife. Animals such as deer and raccoons can be found in most areas. The state's fourteen wildlife refuges include all types of habitats from forests to marshes. Black bears, river otters, bobcats, and many bird species live in remote places such as the Great Dismal Swamp. Virginia Beach is a great location to see pods of dolphins frolicking in the surf. Chesapeake Bay is on the Atlantic flyway, the path that many birds take when traveling south to warmer temperatures for the winter and then traveling north again in spring. In spring and autumn, thousands of migrating birds pause to rest on the area's many islands and on the Eastern Shore. More than two hundred species have been identified, including many kinds of shorebirds. Geese, ducks, and other water birds make their homes in or near Virginia waterways.

The state's bodies of water are home to fish and amphibians. Trout, pike, perch, sunfish, bass, and catfish live in the lakes, rivers, ponds, and streams. Striped bass, American shad, and herring swim through the waters of Chesapeake Bay. Moist land in swamps and near lakes, rivers, and streams is ideal for amphibians such as frogs, salamanders, and newts.

Egrets populate the marshes of Assateague Island.

Atlantic Sturgeon

Black Bear

Blue Crab

1. American Chestnut

This was once the most abundant tree in the hardwood forests of eastern North America, until a chestnut disease killed them all in 1904. Scientists are developing another variety of chestnut tree that they hope will be resistant to the disease.

2. Atlantic Sturgeon

The prehistoric-looking Atlantic Sturgeon was once very common in the Chesapeake. Overfishing and pollution have made this fish nearly extinct. Virginia's James River is one of the last places in which the sturgeon has a stable population.

3. Black Bear

Shenandoah National Park has one of the largest numbers of black bears per square mile of forest. Found throughout the state of Virginia, they are so common that the state allows annual black bear hunting to help control the population.

4. Chesapeake Blue Crab

Also known as the Atlantic blue crab, this tasty crustacean is a vital part of Virginia's commercial fishing industry. Though a female blue crab might lay eight million eggs in her lifetime, their populations are at risk due to habitat loss and overharvesting.

5. Chincoteague Pony

These small horses live on Assateague Island, and some say they are survivors of a sixteenth century Spanish shipwreck. More likely, they descended from horses that the early settlers brought to the island to graze.

6. Eastern Box Turtle

These land-dwelling turtles are easily identified by the bright splashes of orange or yellow on their dark shells. Male box turtles have red eyes, while females have yellow-brown eyes. In the winter, box turtles hibernate in their forest burrows.

7. Lady's Slipper

This delicate plant, with its bright, boot-shaped flowers, grows well in Virginia's moist soil. Lady's slippers go by many different names, including American valerian and moccasin flower. Native Americans and early settlers used it as a drug to help them sleep.

8. River Otter

These playful aquatic mammals have brown fur with patches of silvery gray, a long tail, and short legs. They move comfortably on land but spend most of their time in the water, where their webbed feet help them move swiftly.

9. Virginia Deer

Also known as white tailed deer, or simply whitetails, these large herbivores are common in Virginia's forested areas. They have even invaded the suburbs, wandering into residential yards to feed.

10. Virginia Opossum

Commonly called a possum, these unusual creatures are the only marsupials in Virginia. Their babies are carried and fed inside a special abdominal pouch. When they are old enough to leave the pouch, up to a dozen babies might ride on their mother's back.

Chincoteague Pony

Lady's Slipper

Jamestown transports families back in time.

From the Beginning

The history of Virginia stretches back further than that of any other state. It started out as the first permanent English colony established in the Americas. The history of the land goes back even deeper into the past.

Scientists have established that humans moved into the area now known as Virginia about 16,000 years ago. By about 1400 CE, the descendants of those early people were part of the Woodland American Indian culture that existed throughout the East. The Native Americans who first met Europeans on Virginia's Atlantic coast belonged to groups that spoke Algonquian languages.

The Arrival of Europeans

In the late 1500s, English explorer Sir Walter Raleigh hoped to start a colony in North America. Unlike the pilgrims who traveled to Massachusetts a few decades later, the people bound for Virginia were not looking for religious freedom. They wanted economic opportunity.

Raleigh's first attempt at colonization occurred in 1585 on the island of Roanoke. Life was hard for the settlers, who nearly starved to death. They abandoned the region in 1586, but Raleigh tried again in 1587. Governor John White led the second group to land on Roanoke. He soon went back to England for supplies. When White returned in 1590, he found the settlement empty and no trace of his people. No one knows for sure what happened to the settlers.

In 1606, a group called the Virginia Company received a charter, or contract, from King James of England to establish a colony in Virginia. In May 1607, three ships—the *Susan Constant*, *Godspeed*, and *Discovery*—dropped anchor in a waterway they named the James River. More than one hundred men and boys established the fortified village of Jamestown. In the first years, more than half the colonists died of disease and starvation.

The Jamestown colony survived largely because Captain John Smith took charge. He insisted that every man work and persuaded the nearby Powhatan tribes to help with planting crops. Chief Powhatan had mixed feelings about the settlers. He knew the Europeans could be dangerous, but he also recognized the value of trading with them. For a while, the two groups worked together.

After injuries forced Smith to go back to England, the colony again experienced a "starving time." In spite of these difficulties, more settlers came with more supplies.

Then, around 1612, settler John Rolfe discovered that tobacco grew well in Virginia's climate and could be profitable. Virginians rushed to take more tobacco land from the

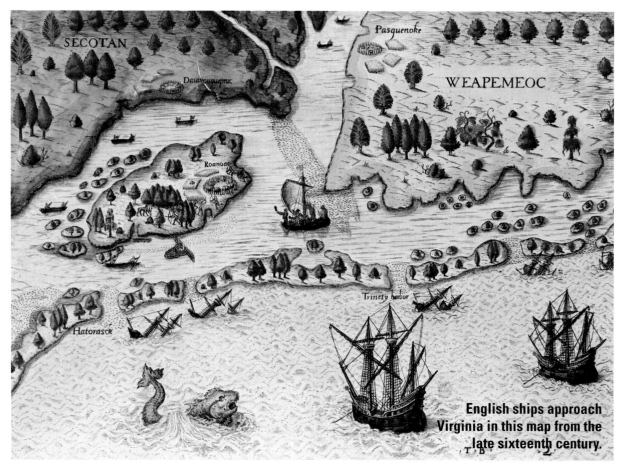

English ships approach Virginia in this map from the late sixteenth century.

Native Americans. Powhatan grew angry when he realized the English had come "not for trade but to invade my people and possess my country." Tensions between the Native Americans and the settlers grew.

Growing Pains

The tobacco trade strained relations between the Native Americans and the colonists. In time, this trade led to suffering for another group—enslaved African Americans. Tobacco profits helped make the Virginia colony a success and plantation owners rich. At first, the planters hired **indentured servants** from England to work the fields. An indentured servant signed a contract, or indenture, to work for three to seven years, in return for their passage to the new world. Many workers hoped to start new lives in the new land after their years of service were over.

In 1619, a Dutch ship brought the first Africans to Virginia. Many other ships carrying Africans who had been captured and forcibly removed from their homeland soon followed. At first, some of the Africans were considered indentured servants. By 1661, however, laws were passed declaring that the new arrivals from Africa were "bound for life." Slavery was official, and indentured servants were no longer needed.

As the Virginia colony prospered, settlers pushed further into Powhatan lands. In the early 1620s, the Native Americans fought back, killing about 350 settlers. In 1624, the English king, Charles I, canceled the Virginia Company's charter and made

Settlers gave thanks after landing at what they called Jamestown in 1607.

The Native People

When the European settlers arrived, there were some fifty thousand members of various tribes in the region. They are divided into three groups based on their language. Groups who spoke the Algonquian language lived on the coast. These include the Croatan tribe, and tribes of the Powhatan Confederacy. The inland Cherokee and Tuscarora tribes spoke Iroquoian languages. The Catawba, Tutelo, and Saponi tribes spoke Sioux dialects. The Yuchi spoke a language that doesn't seem to be related to any other language.

The tribes shared many similarities. They got their food from a combination of hunting (for deer, turkeys, and small game) and agriculture (maize, squash, and beans) as well as some foraging for wild food. Earlier in their cultures, they hunted with spears and atlatls. By the time of European contact they had transitioned to bows and arrows. All of the cultures made pottery, and fashioned clothes and decorative items from leather and woven textiles. There was even trade between the tribes.

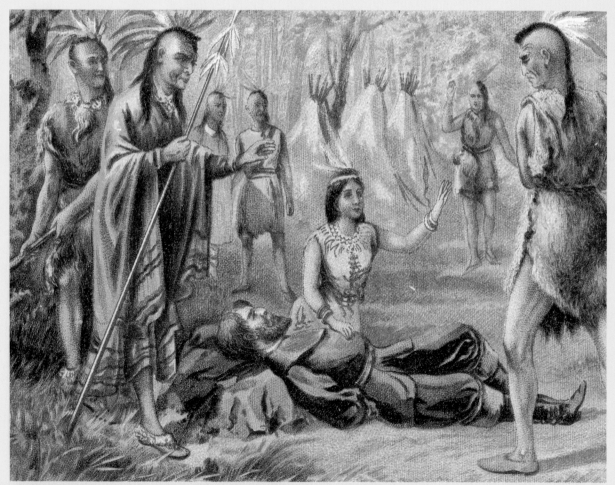

According to the legend of Pocahontas, the daughter of Powhatan saved Captain John Smith from execution.

Tribes in the Powhatan Confederation ruled much of coastal Virginia. Their relations with English settlers varied between friendly and hostile. Later, many of the tribes signed treaties. As more colonists arrived demanding land, though, tensions rose. In the nineteenth century, the tribes were forced off their **reservations** and lost their official status as tribes. Some ended up in Oklahoma, such as the Cherokee and the Yuchi. Others joined with relatives from larger tribes. Among these were the Tuscarora, who went to New York and southern Ontario to join the northern tribes of the Iroquois Confederacy. Some of the Tuscarora live in North Carolina.

Today, the Commonwealth of Virginia recognizes eleven tribes, which are members of, or descendants of, the original groups present at the time of English colonization. They are the Cheroenhaka, Chickahominy, Eastern Chickahominy, Mattaponi, Monacan Nation, Nansemond, Nottoway, Pamunkey, Patawomeck, Rappahannock, and Upper Mattaponi tribes. There are no federally recognized tribes in the state.

Spotlight on the Powhatan Confederation

Paramount Chief Powhatan: Eight of the eleven tribes recognized by Virginia are descendants of the Powhatan Confederation. In the late 1500s and early 1600s, many tribes were united under one strong leader named Wahunsunacawh, who is generally known as Chief Powhatan. Each of the thirty tribes he ruled had their own chief, known as a *weroance* (male) or *weroansqua* (female), but Powhatan was considered the paramount chief, ruling them all.

Food: Duties were mostly divided by gender, with men hunting, and women growing crops of the "**three sisters**"—maize, squash, and beans—and also gathering wild bounty such as nuts. Both men and women probably fished and gathered shellfish.

Houses: The Powhatan peoples built shelters by bending tall, supple saplings into a framework for a domed longhouse. They then covered the frame with mats woven from reeds or grasses, or with bark. Some historians think only the high-ranking members of the tribe had bark coverings, because bark was more scarce and harder to get than reeds.

Villages: The Powhatan tribes moved their entire villages periodically. Without the use of fertilizer or crop rotation, the agricultural land was eventually exhausted. After a while, game, too, became scarce. They would pack up their houses (reusing a lot of the materials) and move to a new, more fertile place.

Virginia America's first royal colony. He also appointed a governor.

More settlers arrived, and by 1700, practically all traces of the Algonquian people were gone. Wars and disease had wiped out many of them. The surviving Native Americans had either given up their traditional ways of life to join white society or moved.

A Thriving and Independent Colony

By the 1770s, Virginia was a thriving colony of about 120,000 people. Many families lived on small farms, but the wealthy plantation owners dominated the economy, social life, and government.

Through the 1600s and 1700s, Virginians had become accustomed to governing themselves. In 1619, they established their own legislature, or law-making body. This legislature, called the House of Burgesses, was one of the first steps toward self-government and democracy in North America.

In 1676, when the royal governor tried to establish tighter control, a colonist named Nathaniel Bacon led an uprising against him. The uprising, called Bacon's Rebellion, did not last long, but it revealed an independent colonial spirit almost one hundred years before the American Revolution.

By the 1750s, some bold pioneers had pushed beyond the mountains into the Ohio River Valley, where they ran into fierce opposition from Native American tribes. The French, who had established a colony in present-day Canada, supported the tribes. The French were also interested in establishing forts and fur-trading outposts in the Ohio Valley. In 1754, George Washington, then a lieutenant colonel in the Virginia militia, led a group of militiamen to establish a fort in what is now western Pennsylvania.

Washington and his men were forced back by the French. That incident was the start of a long war in which Britain, with the help of the Thirteen Colonies and some Native American allies, fought against France and its Native American allies. Known as the French and Indian War (1754–1763), the conflict ended with a British victory. As a result, France lost to Great Britain virtually all the land it had colonized or claimed in North America east of the Mississippi River.

Taxing the Colonies

Great Britain needed money to pay for the war—and to govern its huge empire—so King George III decided to **tax** the colonies. Many colonists were very angry. Any taxes in the past had always been voted on by each colony's legislature, such as Virginia's House of Burgesses. Since the colonists had no representatives in the British legislature, or Parliament, their rallying cry became "No taxation without representation!" The protests continued from the 1760s to 1775. A lot of the action occurred in New England. The Boston Massacre, a skirmish in which British soldiers shot five colonists, took place in 1770. In the Boston Tea Party, colonists protested the British tax on tea by throwing chests of tea from British ships. Those who wanted to dissolve bonds with Britain were called patriots; those who wanted to stay united with Britain were called loyalists.

In September 1774, the First Continental Congress met in Philadelphia. It had delegates from twelve of the thirteen colonies, including Virginia. At the time, delegates hoped to settle their problems with Great Britain peacefully. They were not intent on

Patrick Henry spoke in favor of independence in a famous speech.

"GIVE ME LIBERTY, OR GIVE ME DEATH!"

PATRICK HENRY delivering his great speech on the Rights of the Colonies, before the Virginia Assembly.

Making a "Three Sisters" Garden

Native American tribes in Virginia made use of a system of agriculture known as the "Three Sisters" method. In this system, corn (maize), beans, and squash were planted in one mound. The tall, strong corn stalk provided a structure for climbing bean plants to twine around. The sprawling squash made shade that kept moisture in the soil and kept weeds from growing.

What You Need

Seeds: corn, pole beans, and a squash such as pumpkin

Gardening tools: shovel, spade, etc.

Ruler

Large planter (if you don't have access to a garden)

What To Do

- Choose a planting time after the last frost. Pick a location that gets plenty of sun and has easy access to water from a hose.

- Turn over the soil until it is loose and free of weeds.

- Build a mound of soil about 12 inches (30 cm) high and 18 inches (46 cm) to three feet (1 m) wide. Flatten the top of the mound slightly and make a shallow depression to help hold water.

- Plant the corn first. Soak the corn seeds in water for several hours. Then plant about six seeds in the center of the mound about 6 inches (15 cm) apart, and about one inch (2.5 cm) deep. Water them frequently.

- When the corn is about 6 inches (2.5 cm) tall, remove the smallest or weakest sprouts, leaving three or four remaining.

- Then soak and plant six bean seeds in a circle around the corn, about 6 inches (2.5 cm) away from the corn plants. (They will later be thinned to three to four plants.)

- Soak and plant four squash seeds around the mound. (You will keep only the strongest squash plant.) Water frequently, and keep the mound well formed.

- Harvest your vegetables when they are ready.

independence. Delegates from Virginia included George Washington, Patrick Henry, and Peyton Randolph. Randolph was elected president of the Congress.

In March 1775, the Virginia governor suspended the House of Burgesses. Many representatives continued to meet in a church. At one meeting, the patriot Henry delivered a passionate speech, urging the representatives to take up arms against Britain in self-defense. He ended with the ringing challenge, "I know not what course others may take; but as for me, give me liberty, or give me death!" One month later, fighting broke out at the battles of Lexington and Concord in Massachusetts. When news came of these conflicts, Virginia patriots were ready to fight for independence.

The Fight for Independence

Soon after the outbreak of war, the Second Continental Congress began meeting in Philadelphia in May 1775. Over the months that followed, the Congress made several important decisions. It named George Washington commander of the Continental Army. The delegates also discussed whether they should declare independence from Britain. In June 1776, Virginia delegate and lawyer Richard Henry Lee introduced a resolution asking the Congress to vote for independence.

General George Washington fires the first shot at Yorktown, the decisive battle of the American Revolution.

Another Virginia delegate, Thomas Jefferson, was the main author of the Declaration of Independence. One of the celebrated documents of American democracy, the declaration stated, in clear and eloquent language, the principles that all people are entitled to freedom and equal treatment and that government should serve the people. Based on these principles, the declaration went on to give the reasons why the Thirteen Colonies deserved to be free and independent states. The Congress voted in favor of Lee's resolution on July 2, and it accepted the Declaration of Independence on July 4, 1776.

George Washington kept his ill-equipped army together until, in 1781 and with the help of the French, they trapped the main British army at Yorktown, Virginia. The battered British surrendered, though the war was not officially over until the signing of the Treaty of Paris in 1783.

A New Constitution

The Americans achieved a stable government when representatives met in Philadelphia in 1787 to write a **constitution** for the new nation. James Madison, a representative from Virginia, played a key role in creating the document that established the structure and powers of the U.S. government. The U.S. Constitution was officially approved, or

The issue of slavery divided the states after independence was won.

ratified, in 1788. Many Americans, including Patrick Henry, had opposed the Constitution because they feared a national government that might become too powerful. A handful of patriots, including Madison and Virginian John Marshall, wrote brilliant essays defending the Constitution. That helped persuade enough states to ratify it. Many historians feel that another encouraging factor was George Washington's willingness to serve as the new nation's first president.

The Nation Divides

In the years following independence, Americans wrestled with the basic question of slavery. How could Americans believe in the ideal that "all men are created equal," as Jefferson had written in the Declaration of Independence, yet still allow slavery. By the 1820s, most of the states in the North had **abolished** slavery. In the South, where the plantations needed cheap or free labor, slavery was considered a necessity.

In the first encounter between ironclad ships, the Monitor and the Virginia battle in front of Union troops off of Hampton Roads.

10 KEY CITIES

Naval Station Norfolk

Great Dismal Swamp

James River Bridge to Newport News

1. Virginia Beach: population 447,021

This tourist haven on the Atlantic Ocean at the mouth of Chesapeake Bay is the largest city in Virginia and the thirty-ninth largest in the United States. It has miles of beaches, as well as hundreds of restaurants and hotels.

2. Norfolk: population 245,782

The second largest city in Virginia is part of the Hampton Roads metropolitan area, located on the mouth of the Hampton Roads natural harbor at the mouth of Chesapeake Bay. It is home to the world's largest naval base, Naval Station Norfolk.

3. Chesapeake: population 228,417

Also in the Hampton Roads metropolitan area, Chesapeake is a diverse city where dense urban areas lie beside wilderness such as the Great Dismal Swamp. It was named the twenty-first Best City in America by *Bloomberg BusinessWeek*.

4. Richmond: population 210,309

Virginia's capital, Richmond is located along the James River. The site was an important village during the Powhatan Confederacy in the 1500s, and has remained vital ever since. It served as the capital of the Confederacy during the Civil War.

5. Newport News: population 180,726

Newport News is another city in the Hampton Roads metropolitan area. Though there are several theories, the exact origin of its name is a mystery. Some believe it was named for Christopher Newport, captain of the *Susan Constant*.

VIRGINIA

6. Alexandria: population 146,294

Alexandria is in northern Virginia, close to the nation's capital, Washington DC, and many who live there have government or military jobs. Its historic Old Town district sits on the Potomac waterfront and is home to many fine restaurants and boutiques.

7. Hampton: population 136,836

Located on the southeastern end of the Virginia Peninsula, Hampton is yet another of the seven major cities that make up the Hampton Roads metropolitan area. It is home to Langley Air Force Base, and the new Peninsular Town Center.

8. Roanoke: population 97,469

Roanoke is located in southwest Virginia in the Roanoke Valley. It was formerly called Big Lick, after the natural salt outcropping that formed a salt lick for such local wildlife as deer and (formerly) bison.

9. Portsmouth: population 96,470

Located on the Elizabeth River and part of the Hampton Roads metropolitan area, Portsmouth is home to the Norfolk Naval Shipyard. It has miles of waterfront, and a ferry that transports people between Portsmouth and Norfolk.

10. Suffolk: population 85,181

This city on the Nansemond River is another member of the Hampton Roads metropolitan area. It is known for its peanut production. It is home to Planter's Peanuts, and is the birthplace of Mr. Peanut.

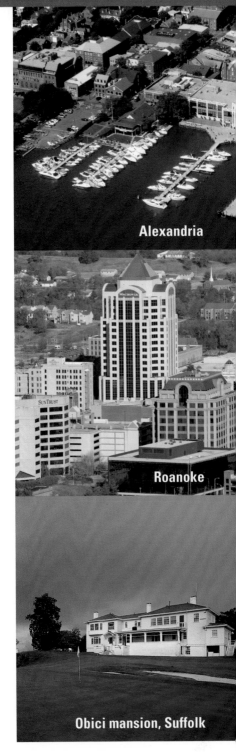

Alexandria

Roanoke

Obici mansion, Suffolk

John Brown's Raid

In 1859, the abolitionist John Brown staged a raid on the Harpers Ferry arsenal. He hoped to distribute the weapons to slaves and encourage them to fight for their freedom. However, the militia captured him and his group. Brown and many of his followers were hanged.

There were also Southerners, including plantation owners, who felt that slavery was wrong, though that did not stop many from keeping their slaves. For some, the decision was purely economic—they could not afford to run their plantations without slave labor. George Washington was one planter who arranged to have his slaves freed after his death. Though he struggled with the question of slavery, Jefferson could not find a solution.

Between 1820 and 1860, the North and the South drifted further apart. Many Virginians, and others in the South, felt that the North was beginning to dominate the nation's economy and government. It seemed that the North's power threatened not just slavery but their entire way of life.

The First Battle of Bull Run, on July 21, 1861, was the first major battle of the Civil War.

One of America's largest slave uprisings took place in Virginia in August 1831. More than forty slaves, led by an enslaved man named Nat Turner, killed fifty-five white people. Many of the rebels, including Turner, were eventually caught and put to death. In the aftermath, white mobs murdered almost two hundred black people, most of whom had nothing to do with the rebellion.

When Abraham Lincoln was elected president in 1860, many Southerners were convinced that

the government would force the end of slavery. At first, seven Southern states—Alabama, Florida, Georgia, Louisiana, Mississippi, South Carolina, and Texas—decided to secede from, or leave, the Union (the United States). They formed an independent nation, the Confederate States of America, which is also known as the Confederacy.

The people of Virginia decided not to leave the Union unless war between the North and South was unavoidable. Confederate forces attacked Fort Sumter in South Carolina in April 1861. President Lincoln then called for volunteers to join the army and fight to reunite the Union. Virginia, along with Arkansas, North Carolina, and Tennessee, decided to join the Confederacy. Richmond was named the capital of the Confederate States of America soon after.

General Robert E. Lee was just one Virginian who struggled with the problem of divided loyalties. Although Lee was a member of Virginia's planter class, he hated slavery. He also believed secession was unconstitutional. A member of the U.S. military, Lee had graduated second in his class from the U.S. Military Academy at West Point. He was a brave and well-respected soldier. By the time the Civil War broke out, Lee had been named the superintendent of West Point. When Lee was offered command of the Union armies, he resigned from the army. He could not bring himself to fight against his native state. Lee joined the Confederate army and became its greatest general.

The people of Virginia's northwestern counties refused to accept the state's decision.

They voted to break away and form the separate state of West Virginia. West Virginia entered the Union in 1863.

Many people believed the war would end quickly in victory for the Union. After all, the North had a larger population than the South and housed three-quarters of the nation's factories and railroads. Southerners, however, believed they were fighting for their way of life and their homes. Many soldiers did not even own slaves. They felt they were fighting off invaders who had attacked their country. The South also had a well-trained cavalry and a number of outstanding generals, many of them Virginians. In fact, the South relied heavily on Virginia because the state had about half the South's weapons, factories, and railroads.

The war lasted four long, bloody years, from 1861 to 1865. Virginia paid a heavy price for its leadership of the Confederacy. Because the Confederate capital was located in Richmond, many battles took place on Virginia soil. More than one hundred battles—one-third of all the fighting—occurred there. Thousands of the state's young men were killed and thousands more crippled. In all, the Civil War claimed more than 600,000 lives. When the war did end in a victory for the North, the states of the Confederacy were brought back into the Union, and slavery was finally abolished throughout the United States, setting four million people free.

Cyrus McCormick's mechanical reaper harvests wheat quickly.

The Modern Age

Much of Virginia's story from the late nineteenth century to the early twenty-first century involves the emergence of modern industries and the development of urban and suburban areas. At the end of the nineteenth century, Virginia had many farming communities and few large cities. Today's Virginia has a small percentage of farming families and many people living in cities or suburbs.

These great changes, shared by all the states, were the result of the **Industrial Revolution** of the nineteenth century. Machines now performed work that, in the past, had depended on human or animal power. In the early 1830s, for example, Virginian Cyrus McCormick invented a mechanical reaper for harvesting wheat. By 1900, McCormick's machines, pulled by tractors, enabled farmers to harvest enormous wheat fields in a single day. Machines allowed farmers to produce more crops with fewer workers.

Recruits for the Civilian Conservation Corps arrive for work preserving Virginia's natural beauty.

Inventions like McCormick's created new industries and new ways of working and living. By the early 1900s, automobiles, electric lights, and telephones contributed to the amazing changes in American life.

Textile mills (factories where cloth was made), long an important part of Virginia's economy, remained important through the early 1900s. New machines helped mills become more productive, but they still required human operators. Unfortunately, the working conditions in these mills were often very bad. Children, men, and women worked long hours for low pay in dark, cramped rooms with little fresh air. In the early 1900s, laws were passed to protect workers and improve conditions in textile mills and other factories.

The Great Depression and Beyond

From 1929 through the 1930s, the entire country suffered through the severe economic times known as the Great Depression. People across the country lost their jobs, their homes, and their belongings. At its height, almost thirteen million people—one-quarter of the nation's workforce—were unemployed.

The government, after Franklin D. Roosevelt was elected in 1932, established programs to help those Americans who needed it most. One program was the Civilian Conservation Corps (CCC). This program employed men to work on highways and bridges, and in forests.

In the 1920s, outsiders who had hiked, camped, hunted, and fished in the Blue Ridge began urging the state and federal governments to turn the region into a park. In 1926, the U.S. Congress authorized the creation of a national park but only if the land was donated. Hundreds of Virginians went to work, urging people to buy 1 acre (0.4 hectare) of Blue Ridge land for six dollars and then donate it to the government. The state government also gained land for the park by buying farms from those who wanted to leave.

Construction on the park began in 1931 when Herbert Hoover, who had a fishing camp in the area, was president of the United States. When President Franklin D. Roosevelt took office in 1933, he also eagerly promoted the park. Hundreds of workers from Virginia and other states went into areas such as the Blue Ridge to harvest lumber or create camping areas and hiking trails.

The CCC sent hundreds of young, unemployed men from Virginia and other states into the Blue Ridge to create camping areas and hiking trails, and to harvest lumber.

The government also paid to relocate more than 450 families who lived in the area. The government made an exception for older residents, allowing them to remain on their land for the rest of their lives. (The last elderly mountain resident died in 1979.)

President Roosevelt dedicated Shenandoah National Park on July 3, 1936. The park is a sanctuary for one hundred varieties of trees and more than one thousand flowering plants. In fact, park personnel say that the Shenandoah has more species of plants than all of Europe. There are 500 miles (800 km) of trails for hiking and horseback riding and dozens of trout streams.

The start of World War II in 1939 also eased some of the effects of the Great Depression. American factories

The Aircraft Warning Service

During World War II, many Virginian civilians—including women and children—were either formally or informally trained to act as aircraft spotters. Particularly along the Virginia coast, these volunteers watched the skies to identify any enemy planes that might be approaching.

The Pentagon was the world's largest office building when it was completed.

were put to work, at first making weapons and equipment for countries in Europe that the United States was helping. When the United States joined the war after Japan bombed the U.S. naval base at Pearl Harbor, Hawaii, in 1941, even more weapons and supplies were needed to support the troops. Virginia's farms and factories produced many wartime supplies. Americans found work in these now-busy factories. Women were encouraged to work in the factories because many men were fighting in the war. Construction on the Pentagon started on September 11, 1941. When it was finished, the Pentagon was the country's largest office building, and at its peak, it housed almost thirty-three thousand workers. On September 11, 2001—exactly sixty years after the groundbreaking ceremony—an airplane hijacked by terrorists hit the Pentagon, killing more than one hundred people inside.

Since World War II, growth and change have continued to characterize life in Virginia. Coastal cities such as Hampton, Newport News, and Virginia Beach have become major population centers. Cities on the western edge of the Piedmont, such as Charlottesville and Roanoke, have also grown. As the federal government has increased in size, more government offices have been located in northeastern Virginia, near Washington, DC, and more people who have jobs in or related to the government have chosen to live in that area. While this growth has been occurring, the people of Virginia are determined to preserve the state's natural beauty and historic sites.

10 KEY DATES IN STATE HISTORY

1. 1585

English explorer Sir Walter Raleigh tries to establish a colony on Roanoke Island. The people of this colony disappeared and their fate remains a mystery.

2. May 14, 1607

Explorers from the Virginia Company of London arrive in Virginia and start to establish Jamestown.

3. May 15, 1776

Virginia declares its independence from Great Britain and adopts its first constitution; Thomas Jefferson writes the Declaration of Independence shortly after.

4. April 30, 1789

George Washington takes office as the nation's first president. He was elected February 4, 1789, in a ballot of the electoral college.

5. April 9, 1865

General Robert E. Lee, a Virginian, surrenders to General Ulysses S. Grant, ending the Civil War, at Appomattox Court House.

6. January 26, 1870

Virginia officials are readmitted to the U.S. Senate and House of Representatives as President Ulysses S. Grant signs the act that ends Reconstruction in the commonwealth.

7. February 2, 1959

Desegregation of the state's public schools begins as African American students, under police protection, enter previously all-white schools in Norfolk and Arlington.

8. January 13, 1990

L. Douglas Wilder of Virginia is sworn in as the first black U.S. governor. He served until 1994, and later served four years as the mayor of Richmond.

9. September 11, 2001

Terrorists fly a hijacked airplane into the Pentagon in Arlington County, Virginia.

10. August 23, 2011

The Virginia Earthquake, magnitude 5.8, damages buildings and is felt in more than twelve states and into Canada.

Native Americans
taught new arrivals
how to grow pumpkins.

3

The People

Some areas of Virginia, especially its urban areas, reflect the country's great mix of peoples and cultures from all parts of the world. In some geographic pockets of the state, however, there is very little diversity. Small communities on some of the Chesapeake Bay and offshore islands remained isolated from the 1600s to the late 1900s. The Chesapeake island of Tangier, for instance, is accessible only by boat or plane. The people there speak in a dialect unique to the area. For example, islanders pronounce *bank* as "bay-eenk." For *chair* and *scared*, they say "churr" and "scurred."

Diversity

The first European settlers in Virginia came from England, and a number of families are still considered FFVs—First Families of Virginia. The Byrd family, for example, established one of the first plantations in the 1600s. Family members have played an important part in the governments of Virginia and West Virginia ever since.

In the 1700s, colonists from other parts of the British Isles and Europe settled mostly in the Tidewater and the Piedmont regions. Farther west, hardy pioneers from Scotland and Ireland made their way south along the Appalachians and settled in the foothills of the Alleghenies and the Blue Ridge Mountains. Like some of the people living on Virginia's eastern islands, several hundred families became isolated in the mountain

Who Virginians Are

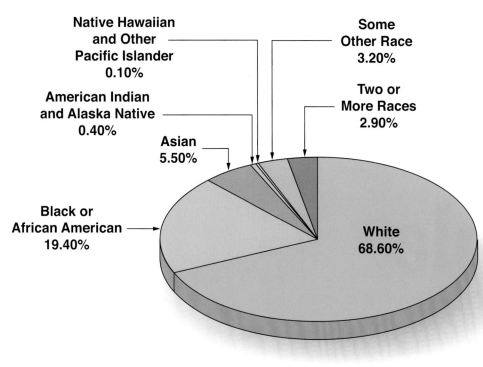

Native Hawaiian and Other Pacific Islander
0.10%

American Indian and Alaska Native
0.40%

Asian
5.50%

Black or African American
19.40%

Some Other Race
3.20%

Two or More Races
2.90%

White
68.60%

**Total Population
8,001,024**

Hispanic or Latino (of any race):

• **631,825 people (7.9%)**
Note: The pie chart shows the racial breakdown of the state's population based on the categories used by the U.S. Bureau of the Census. The Census Bureau reports information for Hispanics or Latinos separately, since they may be of any race. Percentages in the pie chart may not add to 100 because of rounding.

Source: U.S. Bureau of the Census, 2010 Census

valleys. As a result, they developed their own crafts, making furniture, baskets, quilts, and musical instruments.

Throughout much of Virginia's history, people of African descent were largely isolated from the rest of the population. At the time of the Civil War, African Americans made up about 50 percent of the state's population. After 1865, that percentage steadily declined, as thousands of freed slaves headed north and west to look for jobs. The migration slowed in the late 1900s, however. Today, African Americans make up almost 20 percent of the state's population. The proportion of African Americans in the population varies within the state.

Many Virginians today say there are few signs of racial tension between white people and African Americans in spite of the state's history. When the civil rights movement began in the late 1950s, however, some incidents showed that not all Virginians were willing to accept an integrated society. When an African diplomat was refused a room in Virginia hotels because of his race, newspapers around the world reported the story. In 1959, administrators closed public schools in Prince Edward County for five years because they did not want African American children to attend. Since then, Virginia, like many other states in the country, has made many positive changes, including electing African Americans to local and statewide political offices.

Over the past thirty or forty years, Virginia's population has changed to include more people from different parts of the world than ever before. Immigrants come to Virginia from China, Japan, India, and other parts of Asia. There has

also been an increase in Hispanic residents from Mexico, the Caribbean, and Central and South America. These groups have added a cultural richness to life in Virginia.

Native Americans

Before Europeans came to the region, Native Americans were the area's only human inhabitants. Today, however, they make up less than one percent of the population. The

Old ways of doing things were preserved by isolated settlers in the Blue Ridge Mountains.

10 KEY PEOPLE ★ ★

Arthur Ashe

Sandra Bullock

Katie Couric

1. Arthur Ashe

A Richmond native, born in 1943, Arthur Ashe was eight years old when he began playing tennis, when many competitions did not allow African Americans. Ashe won the 1968 U.S. Open and 1975 Wimbledon tournament, the first African American player to win both.

2. Tiki and Ronde Barber

These twin brothers grew up in Roanoke, and both went on to become stars in the National Football League. Tiki was a running back for the New York Giants. Ronde was a cornerback for the Tampa Bay Buccaneers. Both brothers are now sports broadcasters.

3. Sandra Bullock

This Arlington native appeared in such movies as *Speed* and *Miss Congeniality*. Later, the actress won an Oscar for her role in the 2009 movie *The Blind Side*. In 2012, she was listed as the world's highest-paid actress.

4. Richard E. Byrd

Richard E. Byrd, born in Winchester in 1888, served as a navy pilot in World War I. In 1926, Byrd made the first flight over the North Pole. Three years later he flew over the South Pole.

5. Katie Couric

Born in Arlington in 1957, this groundbreaking television news reporter became the first woman to anchor the evening news alone on the *CBS Evening News* in 2006. She switched to the Web when Yahoo named her its global anchor in 2014.

6. Ella Fitzgerald

Born in Newport News in 1917, she got her big break in New York at amateur night at the Apollo Theater in Harlem. Fitzgerald was considered, by the age of twenty, one of the best singers in the country.

Ella Fitzgerald

7. Thomas Jonathan "Stonewall" Jackson

Born in Clarksburg in 1824, General Stonewall Jackson received his nickname in July 1861, during the First Battle of Bull Run. As Confederate troops were retreating, one of the officers cried out, "Look at Jackson—he's standing like a stone wall!"

8. Henrietta Lacks

This African American woman made medical history by being the unwitting donor of what became the first immortal human cell line for medical research. Scientists have grown more than 20 tons of her cells for studies about cancer, HIV, gene mapping, and more.

Stonewall Jackson

9. Wanda Sykes

This comedian, writer, actress, and voice talent was born in Portsmouth. In 2009, Sykes was the first African American woman, as well as the first gay person, to be the featured entertainer at the White House Correspondents' Association dinner.

10. Pharrell Williams

This singer, songwriter, record producer, and fashion designer was born in Virginia Beach. A successful soundtrack producer, he also wrote the soundtrack to the movie *Despicable Me*.

Wanda Sykes

state has only two reservations—one is occupied by the Pamunkeys, and the other by the Mattaponis. Both groups are part of the Powhatan Confederacy. The Monacans recently won ownership of their ancestral lands on Bear Mountain.

The Pamunkey reservation is on the Pamunkey River. It includes about 1,200 acres (490 ha) of land. Almost thirty families live on the reservation. Other Pamunkeys live in nearby cities and towns. There used to be a Pamunkey school on the reservation, but now most Pamunkey children attend the public schools in King William County. The Pamunkeys have their own tribal government made up of a chief and seven council members. Elections are held every four years. The tribal government is responsible for upholding the laws that the Pamunkeys have established.

Members of the Mattaponi wear traditional dress when they gather for a powwow on their reservation.

The reservation also includes the Pamunkey Indian Museum, which documents and celebrates the Pamunkeys' history in the state. These people are well known for their pottery, beadwork, and other art. They sell some of their impressive artwork to support the community, but most is created to honor Pamunkey traditions.

The Mattaponis trace their heritage directly to Powhatan, the great chief and father of Pocahontas. The Mattaponi reservation, one of the oldest in the country, was established in 1658. Located near the Mattaponi River, it covers about 150 acres (60 ha). More than four hundred people are officially part of the Mattaponi tribe, but fewer than a quarter of them live on the reservation. The Mattaponis also have their own government, including a chief, an assistant chief, and seven council members.

In 1646, the Mattaponis paid tribute to the Virginia governor. This old tradition continues today. Every year, on the fourth Wednesday of November, the tribe gives a gift of fish or game to the governor of the commonwealth.

Their reservation houses a fish hatchery and marine science center. The American shad is a fish important to the Mattaponis' diet and culture. At the center, Mattaponis monitor shad populations and water quality. They also develop educational resources that help communities protect their land and water.

Give and Take

The Pamunkey have a tradition that when you take a fish from the water, you must give something back. Inspired by this, the Pamunkey established a fish hatchery in 1918 to raise young shad and release them into the water. This helped keep the Pamunkey River healthy and full of fish.

Sixteen men who signed the Declaration of Independence were educated at the College of William and Mary.

Education in Virginia

Education is an important issue for many Virginians. The state has been one of the nation's leaders in higher education. For example, the College of William and Mary, founded in Williamsburg in 1693, is the country's second-oldest college. In 1819, the University of Virginia was established in Charlottesville, largely thanks to the work of Thomas Jefferson. The Virginia Military Institute, founded in 1839, is the nation's oldest state-supported military college. In 1868, the Hampton Normal and Agricultural Institute (now Hampton University) was created to prepare African American men and women to teach newly freed people.

Virginia's public schools for elementary and secondary school children, however, did not develop as early or as quickly. A law establishing public schools in Virginia was not passed until 1846—two hundred years after Massachusetts passed a similar law.

Virginia has made great strides in educating all of its students.

Even then, the Virginia law was not strongly enforced. There were various reasons for this lack of interest in public education. Until the Civil War era, plantation owners hired tutors for their children or operated small schools for local white children. Local church congregations also established their own schools. Over time, however, Virginia did establish public school systems throughout the state.

In the 1960s, studies showed that Virginia's public schools ranked below the national average. Educators and parents worked to raise the schools' rankings. They formed committees to improve courses and pressed the state government for money to modernize facilities and increase pay for teachers. The determination of educators, parents, students, and legislators has paid off. According to the National Center for Education Statistics, Virginia's math and reading scores beat the national average every year from 1992 to 2013. While there is still more to do, this example shows how Virginians can work together to improve their state.

10 KEY EVENTS ★

George Washington's Birthday Celebration

Mattaponi Indian Reservation Powwow

1. 100 Miles of Lights

From November through early January, seven Virginia cities— Richmond, Williamsburg, Newport News, Hampton, Norfolk, Portsmouth, and Virginia Beach—join to celebrate the season with holiday light shows, parades on land and water, festivals, caroling, musical events, and food.

2. American Music Festival

For the past twenty years, this Virginia Beach festival has been the largest outdoor music event on the East Coast. Every Labor Day weekend, more than thirty acts gather to perform on a huge beachfront stage for a three-day celebration.

3. George Washington's Birthday Celebration

Since the American Revolution, people in Alexandria have been celebrating George Washington's birthday. Every February, they mark the occasion with reenactments of historic events, parades, music, and balls. Celebrations also take place at Washington's home, Mount Vernon.

4. Hampton Bay Days

Every September, Hampton plays host to one of the largest family-oriented festivals on the East Coast. In addition to music on three stages, the event has food, fireworks, the Freaky Kon Tiki River Raft Race, and a play-and-learn area for kids.

5. Mattaponi Indian Reservation Powwow

Every May or June in King William County, the Mattaponi tribe celebrates 10,000 years of history with its annual powwow— the only one in Virginia that takes place on a reservation.

6. Neptune Festival

In Virginia Beach at the end of September, this festival features surfing competitions, sand sculpting, arts and crafts, and three stages of entertainment. At the same time, the Boardwalk Art Show and Festival showcases art and food along the historic boardwalk.

7. Reenactment of the Battle of New Market

In May, volunteers, including many teens, reenact the 1864 Civil War battle in which cadets from the nearby Virginia Military Institute in Lexington fought against Union soldiers. The reenactment occurs on the battle site, which is part of a state historic park.

8. Richmond Folk Festival

This free, three-day festival in October celebrates Virginia's rich and diverse folk history with traditional crafts, food, dancing, and music. Seven stages hold continuous performances, while throughout the event reenactors give demonstrations of old-time activities and living history.

9. Shenandoah Apple Blossom Festival

Every April, more than 250,000 people flock to the Shenandoah Valley to take part in a festival that includes races, dances, parades, band competitions, and a circus. One of the highlights is the coronation of Queen Shenandoah.

10. Virginia State Fair

The State Fair is held every year at the end of September in Caroline County at the Meadow Event Park. It has games, rides, agriculture and livestock exhibits, and such fair food as corn dogs, funnel cakes, and more.

Neptune Festival

Battle of Newmarket

The Virginia State Capitol is located in Richmond.

How the Government Works

O On June 29, 1776, Virginia became an independent commonwealth when its representatives adopted its first constitution. The constitution established an executive branch, two legislative houses, and a judicial department. The most important part of the constitution, however, was its Declaration of Rights.

Many of the ideas in Virginia's constitution later made their way into the U.S. Constitution. This is not surprising because a large part of both documents was written by the same man, Virginian George Mason. He wrote the Declaration of Rights. As a representative at the 1787 convention at which the U.S. Constitution was written, Mason worried about giving too much power to the federal government. He successfully argued to add a Bill of Rights. The first ten amendments to the U.S. Constitution, called the Bill of Rights, guarantee Americans important freedoms, including the freedoms of speech and religion. They also give Americans protection from unfair treatment by the government. Mason's efforts earned him the nickname Father of the Bill of Rights.

Throughout the state's history, Virginians have been willing to make changes to their government when needed. The 1776 state constitution has gone through five major revisions. Other changes have been achieved by a simple act of the general assembly (the state legislature). In colonial times, for example, the Episcopal Church was the state's official church, but many people felt this was not fair to those who followed other religions or no religion. Thomas Jefferson devised a new law, the Virginia Statute for Religious Freedom, that guaranteed freedom of worship for all. Jefferson's law has been a model for other state constitutions.

A more recent example of how Virginia alters its government to accommodate changing times relates to the state supreme court. The general assembly appointed a commission to look for ways to help the Virginia supreme court, which was being overwhelmed by too many cases. The state legislators suggested adding another court to hear appeals (requests for a court decision to be reviewed). This court of appeals would decide some of the cases. The supreme court would get the cases that involved a more complicated interpretation of the state constitution. The new court, called the court of appeals, went into effect in 1985. It has helped relieve the pressure on the state's highest court.

There is seating for one hundred in the House of Delegates in the state Capitol Building.

Government of the People

Most Virginians believe that the structure of their government should be as simple as possible to respond to the needs of the people. To bring government close to the people, the voters in each of the ninety-five counties elect a board of supervisors to handle most local matters. Each town sends a supervisor to the county board. There are thirty-eight cities, which are usually governed by a mayor and city council. In Virginia, cities are independent from counties. Independent cities have their own governments and levy their own taxes. Cities can vote to become towns, thereby dissolving their own governments and becoming a part of the country. Bedford is the last city to do that, becoming a town on July 1, 2013.

All levels of the Virginia government work to help businesses. The Department of Economic Development, for example, which operates out of the governor's office, works with business groups to attract new opportunities to the state.

The state government serves a similar function for the arts. This involvement began in

Legislators register their votes on a proposal in 2010.

1936, during the Great Depression. To help the many artists who were out of work, the general assembly created the Virginia Museum of the Fine Arts—the country's first state-supported museum of the arts. The museum provided a place for artists to display their work. It also established a performing arts program, providing funds to support performances by local theater groups, symphony orchestras, and dance companies.

In addition to state and local government, Virginia is represented in the U.S. Congress in Washington, DC. Like all other states, Virginia has two U.S. senators who serve six-year terms. As of 2014, the state had eleven representatives in the U.S. House of Representatives. Representatives serve two-year terms. A state's population determines its number of representatives.

Three State Branches

Executive

The governor, lieutenant governor, and state attorney general are elected for four-year terms. The governor's major job is to see that the laws are carried out. He or she appoints the directors of executive departments, such as education and transportation, who oversee the day-to-day work of the government. The governor can also propose new laws and can reject laws passed by the general assembly. Virginia is the only state in which the governor cannot serve two consecutive terms.

Legislative

The law-making body is the general assembly, made up of two houses—a forty-member senate, elected for four-year terms, and a house of delegates, with one hundred members elected for two-year terms.

Judicial

There are four levels of courts. The Virginia supreme court with its seven judges is the highest state court. The state supreme court hears appeals of decisions made by the lower courts. Below the supreme court is the court of appeals. Below that are the thirty-one judicial circuits that deal with general court matters, trying both criminal cases and civil cases, in which someone seeks damages from a company or an individual. The fourth—and lowest—level is made up of special courts, such as juvenile courts or family courts.

How a Bill Becomes a Law

As in other states, before a law is passed in Virginia, it goes through an established process. Most laws begin with a suggestion or an idea from a Virginia resident or a member of the state legislature. The proposed law is called a bill.

When a legislator in one of the two legislative houses introduces a bill, it is assigned to a committee, which may revise or reject the bill. If the committee is satisfied with the bill, it presents it to the entire house. The bill is read to the house three times. After the second reading, legislators can amend—or revise—the bill. They usually debate the bill after the third reading. Then the legislators vote on the bill. If it is approved, it is sent to the other house, where it goes through a similar process.

If both houses agree on the bill, it is sent to the governor. If the governor approves the bill, he or she can sign it into law. The governor can also make changes to the bill and send it back to the general assembly. If the governor does not take any action, the bill will automatically become law after a certain amount of time. The governor can also veto—or reject—the bill. The vetoed bill can still become law if two-thirds of the members of both houses vote to override the governor's veto.

The extent of the ability of the governor to use his veto power was tested in June 2014. Governor Terry McAuliffe wanted to veto individual items in the state budget. One of his goals was to expand health coverage under the Affordable Care Act. To do that, he wanted to veto an amendment to the state budget that said that Medicaid —which is how health insurance would be extended to the poor—could not be expanded unless the legislature allocated money just for that purpose. Virginia House Speaker William J. Howell found a rule that prevented the governor from doing what he wanted, and the legislature then passed a two-year budget.

Some members of the legislature argued that what the governor had tried to do was not allowed under the state constitution. The Virginia constitution requires the legislature to approve any spending, even if the money is coming from the federal government to pay for most of the Medicaid expansion. Other legislators wanted the issue debated, and the governor promised to explore other ways to expand health coverage.

Still to be worked out is who was right, the governor or the leader of the house.

POLITICAL FIGURES
FROM VIRGINIA

Eric Cantor:
United States Representative, 2001-2014

This representative from the state's seventh district was the House Majority Leader, a powerful position, when he lost the Republican primary to David Brat in June 2014. He resigned that position shortly after rather than hold it to the end of his term.

Thomas Jefferson:
United States President, 1801-1809

Born in Shadwell in 1743, he served as governor of Virginia, U.S. secretary of state, and vice president before becoming the nation's third president. His tombstone lists just three of his contributions: "author of the Declaration of American Independence, of the Statute [law] of Virginia for religious freedom, and father of the University of Virginia."

Toddy Puller:
United States Senator, 1999-

Linda Todd "Toddy" Puller is a Democrat who was a member of the Virginia House of Delegates from 1992 to 1999, and a member of the Virginia Senate from 1999 to the present. She suffered a stroke several years ago and has partial paralysis on one side of her body. She strongly supports veterans' issues.

VIRGINIA ★★★★★
YOU CAN MAKE A DIFFERENCE

Contacting Lawmakers

Every citizen can help make a difference in politics, legislation, and lawmaking in a variety of ways. People who are over eighteen years of age can vote for representatives who will support the things they believe in and enact laws they endorse. People of all ages can participate in other ways. One of the best ways to let your opinion be known is by contacting elected officials.

The web site **www.virginia.gov** is full of information about Virginia government, including instructions for contacting members of all branches.

Citizens can find out how to call or email the governor at **governor.virginia.gov/about/contact-us**

To find out who your local representatives are, and how to contact them, visit: **conview.state.va.us/whosmy.nsf/VGAMain?openform**

From Tragedy to a New Bill

Sometimes, legislators have to rely on citizens to bring issues to their attention. Too often, it is a tragedy that reveals the need for change. On October 5, 2012 a young Virginia State Trooper named Andrew Fox was directing traffic on a special detail outside of King's Dominion theme park and the State Fair. As he attempted to stop traffic, one driver didn't see him and struck him with her SUV. Andrew Fox was dragged down the highway and killed.

That driver's only penalty was a one-year suspended sentence. This didn't sit well with many people. The victim's family started a petition drive. Signing a petition is one way you can express support for a new proposal. They wanted much tougher penalties for anyone who kills a law enforcement officer while driving recklessly.

Many people began writing letters to their representatives. The proposed "Andrew's Law" went to Facebook, garnering even more support. Finally, the legislation was drafted as Senate Bill 293.

Though the bill was delayed until 2015, the senate considered whether the bill should be expanded to include harsher penalties for a person who is driving recklessly when they cause the death of *anyone*—not just a law enforcement officer.

Virginia is a leader in
breeding horses.

Making a Living

T he mix of industries in Virginia reveals the same blending of old and new that exists in so much of the state's life. Some people work in traditional occupations such as farming and fishing. Others spend their time exploring Virginia's past by working at one of the many historic sites. Still others are engaged in manufacturing, research, or providing services. Service workers include people in a wide range of jobs, such as government employees, teachers, healthcare workers, and staff at hotels, restaurants, and shops as well as all the tourist sites.

Agriculture

For much of Virginia's history, most families lived by farming. Today, far fewer people are engaged in agriculture. Still, the state has more than forty-seven thousand farms on 8.5 million acres (3.4 million ha) of farmland. Almost 90 percent of the farms are family owned. The state has more than 1,200 "Century Farms"—farms in operation for one hundred years or more. Soybeans, corn, and tobacco are among the biggest cash crops. Soybeans are used in many products, including tofu, oil, soap, and crayons. The corn grown in Virginia is used mostly for grain to feed livestock.

Rockingham County in the Shenandoah Valley is one of the nation's largest turkey-raising centers. The state ranked fifth in the nation in 2012 for turkey production.

10 KEY INDUSTRIES

Agriculture

1. Agriculture

Agriculture is Virginia's largest industry, producing revenue of about $52 billion for the state every year. It also provides about 311,000 jobs for the state. There are more than forty-seven thousand farms. Horse breeding is also a major part of Virginia's agricultural revenue.

2. Automotive

This industry accounts for 7 percent of all manufacturing employment in Virginia. One of the largest companies is Volvo Trucks, whose 1.6 million square foot (111,484 sq. km) New River Valley Plant assembles all Volvo trucks sold in North America and is the largest Volvo truck plant in the world.

New River Valley Plant

3. Energy

Virginia is heavily involved with all aspects of energy production, from coal mining to utilities feeding the grid, to nuclear plants. It has about 130 power plants that use coal, biomass, nuclear, natural gas, or hydropower to produce electricity.

4. Fishing Industries

With miles of coastline on Chesapeake Bay and the Atlantic Ocean, as well as numerous rivers, fishing and related industries provide major revenue for Virginia. Some of the major commercial species are scallops, clams, crabs, flounder, and oysters.

5. Food Processing

Virginia has 580 food processing companies, which provide jobs to nearly 40,000 people. Some of the biggest processing companies in Virginia are Smithfield (known for its hams), and Perdue (famous for chickens).

Smithfield Ham

VIRGINIA ★ ★ ★ ★ ★

6. Government

Positioned so close to the nation's capital, Washington, DC, Virginia is home to many government employees. In addition to military installations, it is home to the Pentagon, which employs approximately thirty-one thousand personnel, both military and civilian.

7. Health Care

Components of the health care industry include institutions such as hospitals, nursing homes, and private medical facilities, as well as medical insurance companies and manufacturers of medical equipment.

8. Military

In addition to training military personnel, military facilities provide jobs for many Virginians. The major bases include Quantico, Norfolk Naval Base, Fort Eustis, and Fort Monroe.

9. Technology

Virginia has a higher concentration of technology workers than any other state in the U.S. Computer chips are one of the state's highest-grossing exports. Virginia also has strong biotechnology and nanotechnology industries.

10. Tourism and Hospitality

In 2012, tourism brought $21.2 billion in visitor spending, and supported 210,000 jobs. Virginia has many popular tourist destinations, from the fun-in-the-sun favorite Virginia Beach, to the scenic Shenandoah Valley.

Old Point Comfort Lighthouse at Fort Monroe

Tourism

However, chickens are Virginia's most valuable agricultural product. Cattle also play an important role in Virginia's agricultural industry. Beef is the second-largest commodity in the state, and milk is the third.

Virginia is also well known for its horse farms in the northwestern part of the state. In fact, Triple Crown winner Secretariat was born in Doswell. Home to 170,000 horses, Virginia is the fifth-largest equine state in the nation.

Virginia's wineries attracted 1.6 million visitors in 2010. Two years later, Virginia was named one of the ten best wine travel destinations by Wine Enthusiast magazine.

Gifts from the Water

Since the earliest days of Jamestown, Virginians have relied on products from the Atlantic Ocean and Chesapeake Bay. Today, crab and oyster farms are scattered along the jagged shore of the bay. Shellfish, such as oysters, clams, and the famous blue crabs, are an important part of the commercial fishing industry. Flounder, bass (called rockfish in the Chesapeake region), and a number of other fish also thrive in Virginia waters. Offshore, many sea clams and scallops are harvested. Fishermen catch large ocean fish, such as

The blue crab is one of the greatest resources in Virginia's waters.

swordfish and tuna, on baited hooks pulled close to the surface. These fishing lines can be 40 to 50 miles (65 to 80 km) long.

One important type of fish is menhaden. The Algonquian Native Americans called it munnawhatteaug, which means "fertilizer." They used the menhaden to fertilize their crops—a technique they taught to the early settlers.

Smithfield Hams

The beautifully restored town of Smithfield is famous not only as a historic seaport but as the birthplace of the Smithfield hams. Now a subsidiary of a company from China, these hams are sold throughout the world.

Today, people in small aircraft spot schools of menhaden and radio the locations to fishing boats. Fishers then catch the menhaden in large nets. As in colonial times, people do not eat the fish but use it for fertilizer. People also feed menhaden to their livestock, make fishing bait out of it, and use its oil to produce food, paint, and cosmetics.

Menhaden is used mostly as animal feed and fertilizer.

Recipe for Boiled Virginia Peanuts

Virginia has more than two hundred peanut farmers, who grow more than five million pounds (2,267,961 kg) of peanuts a year. A fourteen-year-old Virginia boy even won a contest by designing the famous "Mr. Peanut" of Planters Peanuts fame. Boiled peanuts are a favorite snack in Virginia and throughout the South. Most whole, raw peanuts—the kind used in boiled peanuts—are of a variety called the Virginia peanut. Peanuts are a high protein snack. Though boiled peanuts are very salty, the boiling transfers healthy antioxidants from the shells to the meat, making them four times higher in antioxidants than raw or roasted peanuts.

What You Need

3–5 pounds (1.4–2.3 kg) of raw peanuts in their shells

1 cup (237 milliliters) of salt

A large pot

Enough water to cover the peanuts

Optional: seasoning such as Old Bay Seasoning, garlic, or cayenne pepper to taste

What to Do

1. If you can, find green peanuts, which are sometimes available in grocery stores. If not, use any raw peanuts. (Do not use roasted peanut—they won't work for boiling.) If you use raw peanuts, they must be rehydrated. Soak them in a bowl of water overnight, then proceed with cooking.

2. Put the peanuts in the pot and then fill the pot with enough water to completely cover the peanuts. Boil the peanuts on high for about three hours.

3. Some of the water will boil off. To avoid cooling the mixture during cooking, boil additional water in another small pot and add it as needed to keep the peanuts covered. When done, the shells (which are not eaten) will be soft and the nuts inside will be very tender.

4. Leftover peanuts should be refrigerated if they will be eaten within a few days, or frozen for up to a year.

A Changing Economy

The twentieth century saw major changes in Virginia's economic life. World War II, in particular, spurred the state's role in shipbuilding and in training bases for the military services. After the government hired the Newport News Shipbuilding and Dry Dock Company to build aircraft carriers and other warships for the U.S. Navy, it became the world's largest shipbuilding company.

Since parts of Virginia are very close to Washington, DC, it is not surprising that the federal government is the employer of many Virginians. The headquarters for several government agencies are located in northern Virginia, including the Department of Defense (at the Pentagon), the U.S. Patent and Trademark Office, the U.S. Fish and Wildlife Service, the Central Intelligence Agency (CIA), and the National Science Foundation. Many Virginians commute to work in Washington, DC.

Historic Sites

Visitors to Virginia can enjoy historical experiences at a number of magnificent plantations and the homes of famous Americans, including Washington's Mount Vernon and Jefferson's Monticello. Jefferson's talent as an architect is also on display in the buildings of the University of Virginia in Charlottesville, and the Virginia State Capitol in Richmond.

In fact, no state in the nation has more historic sites than Virginia, including early homes, plantations, and battlefields dating from the American Revolution and the Civil War. Restoring and preserving these sites, along with providing guided tours and other services to visitors, adds to Virginia's tourism industry, which supports more than 200,000 jobs and generates almost $19 billion in spending. Some of the money people spend while visiting Virginia's sites, staying at hotels, eating at restaurants, and shopping in stores goes to the state government in the form of taxes.

In 1926, a Virginia reverend named Dr. W. A. R. Goodwin shared with American philanthropist John D. Rockefeller Jr. his dream of preserving Williamsburg's historic

Weird Attractions

Virginia offers some decidedly offbeat tourist attractions. Foamhenge in Natural Bridge is a replica of Stonehenge made entirely out of foam. In Fredericksburg, visitors can see the grave of Stonewall Jackson's amputated arm. [The rest of him is buried elsewhere.]

Mount Vernon, the home of George Washington, is a popular site for tourists.

buildings. Rockefeller agreed that an important part of the nation's early history might soon be lost forever. He gave money to help restore and develop Colonial Williamsburg, which today encompasses about 85 percent of Virginia's original capital city. The site includes eighty-eight restored eighteenth-century structures as well as scores of reconstructed homes, shops, taverns, and government buildings.

More than twenty battlefield sites from the Civil War add to Virginia's tourism industry. The most popular sites for visitors include Manassas—known to Northerners as Bull Run—where the Confederates won two victories, and the village of Appomattox Court House. It was there, at McClean House, that General Lee surrendered to Union general Ulysses S. Grant. Many other sites are located between Washington, DC, and Richmond, and in the Shenandoah Valley.

Natural Wonders

Tourists also visit the state to enjoy its natural wonders. Many families enjoy camping in the state and national parks. The rivers, lakes, and streams offer great boating, swimming, and fishing. Many people go to Chesapeake Bay to enjoy the abundant water activities.

Virginia Beach is another popular tourist destination. It is said that this resort city has the longest pleasure beach in the world. Virginia Beach includes 35 miles (56 km) of waterfront property, a 3-mile (5-km) boardwalk, and plenty of entertainment, from restaurants and shops to live music. Birding trails, whale-watching expeditions, golf courses, and fishing competitions are other fun recreational offerings.

From its farms and waters to its historical sites and bustling cities, the Old Dominion is full of opportunities for Virginians and visitors. Virginia's economy draws strength from the land, the people, and their history.

Wild ponies swim ashore on Chincoteague Island.

VIRGINIA

Winchester   Leesburg
                        Chesapenke & Ohio Canal
                        National Historic
                    Manassas
                    National
                    Battlefield
                    Park
            Front   Arlington
            Royal
        Luray
        CAVERNS   Manassas   Alexandria
Blue   Shenandoah   Mount
Grass   George   National   Vernon
        Washington   Park   George
        National   Washington
        Forest   Harrisonburg   Birthplace
                                          National
                    Charlottesville   Monument   New
        Staunton   Church

Covington   Monticello   Zoar   Reedville   Tangier
                    LAKE   State
        Lexington MONTICELLO   Forest
        NATURAL   George   Buckingham-   Belle Isle
        BRIDGE   Washington Appomattox   State Park
                   National   State Forest
Big   Pocahontas Forest   Richmond
Rock   New
        Roanoke   Appomattox   PAMUNKEY   Point
Bluefield   Court House   RESERVATION
Jefferson Blacksburg Booker T. National   Williamsburg
National   Washington Historic Park Petersburg Newport Kiptopeke
Forest   National   Petersburg   News
        Pulaski   Monument   National   Norfolk   Hampton
                    Fairy   Battlefield Portsmouth Virginia
        Marion   Stone   Beach
    Mount Rogers   State   Chesapeake
    National   Park   Back Bay National
    Recreation   Wildlife Refuge
    Area   Philpott   Martinsville   Emporia
Cumberland Gap   Lake
National   Galax   Great
Historic   Occoneechee Dismal
Park   Bristol   State Park Swamp
Wilderness Road   Danville   National
State Park   Palmer Wildlife
Ewing   Springs Refuge

Legend:

	Interstate Highway
	U.S. Highway
	State Highway
	State Capital
	City or Town
	Indian Reservation
	Highest Point in the State
	Mountains
	State Park
	National Forest
	State Forest
	National Park
	Historic Park
	National Monument
	Wildlife Refuge
	National Seashore
	Battlefield
	Recreation Area
	National Memorial
	Blue Ridge Parkway & Sky Line Drive

miles
0   20

ATLANTIC OCEAN

VIRGINIA ★ ★ ★ ★ ★
MAP SKILLS

1. What is the capital of Virginia?

2. This large, famous bay encompasses most of Virginia's coastline.

3. What is the major city closest to Arlington?

4. Name the westernmost major city pictured on this map.

5. Name the two northernmost cities pictures on this map.

6. This swamp on the border of Virginia and North Carolina is one of the premier natural places in the state.

7. This mountain chain runs along the northwest border of Virginia

8. These mountains, southeast of the Appalachians, run through Virginia's interior.

9. This major interstate runs north-south and passes through Richmond, the capital.

10. Name three cities that are closest to the border with North Carolina.

Richmond

Ewing

10. Palmer Springs, Bristol, and Ewing
9. Interstate 95
8. The Blue Ridge Mountains
7. The Appalachian Mountains
6. The Great Dismal Swamp
5. Winchester and Leesburg
4. Ewing
3. Alexandria
2. Chesapeake Bay
1. Richmond

State Flag, Seal, and Song

Virginia's flag shows the state coat of arms on a blue background.

Virginia's state seal has two sides: a front and a back. The front shows Virtus, the Roman goddess of virtue, dressed as a warrior. She is standing with her left foot on the chest of a defeated warrior meant to represent tyranny. Virtus symbolizes the spirit of Virginia, and tyranny represents Great Britain. The bottom of the seal shows the state's motto. Translated from Latin, it means "Thus Always to Tyrants." The back of the seal shows three Roman goddesses representing liberty, eternity, and fruitfulness. They stand below the word Perservando, which means "by persevering."

"Carry Me Back to Old Virginia" by James Bland was the state song from 1940 until the general assembly senate decided to make it the state song emeritus in 2001. One of the objections was over its romantic view of slavery. There have been suggestions for replacements, but as of 2014 no song had been chosen. To learn the lyrics to the former state song, visit

www.statesymbolsusa.org/Virginia/Virginia-state-song.html

Virginia's flag is blue with the state seal in the center.

Glossary

abolish	To completely do away with, as in the abolition of slavery.
bay	A draft of a proposed law that has to be approved by a legislative body.
bill	A draft of a proposed law that has to be approved by a legislative body.
blaze	To mark a trail by making cuts in a tree.
CE	Common Era, a method of calculating time using an agreed-upon year-zero. (BCE = Before Common Era.)
constitution	A written system of principles and laws laid out for running the government.
estuary	A partially enclosed area where fresh river waters and salty ocean waters meet.
fertile	Able to produce a large amount of crops; supporting life.
indentured servant	A person who sells himself or herself into service for a fixed period, usually between three and seven years, often in exchange for transportation to a new land.
Industrial Revolution	A rapid change in the economy started by the introduction of power-driven machinery, which changed manufacturing.
paramount	Of the highest rank, the most important.
plantation	A large estate or farm, which can often operate almost like a village, with live-in laborers.
reservation	An area of land reserved for the use of Native American tribes.
slave	A person who is owned by another person and bound to serve for life.
stalactite	A cave formation hanging from the cave roof caused by dripping mineral-rich water (unlike stalagmites, which grow from the floor up.)
tax	Money that the government collects based on income or assets, which is used to support the government.
three sisters	A planting method using corn (maize), beans, and squash all planted close together.

More About Virginia

BOOKS

Greenberg, Ben. *Natural Virginia*. Charlottesville, VA: University of Virginia Press, 2014.

King, David C. *The Powhatan*. New York, NY: Marshall Cavendish Benchmark, 2008.

Miller, Lee. *Roanoke: The Mystery of the Lost Colony*. New York, NY: Scholastic, 2007.

Trueit, Trudi Strain. *Thomas Jefferson*. New York, NY: Marshall Cavendish Benchmark, 2009.

WEBSITES

Colonial Williamsburg:
www.colonialwilliamsburg.com

The Official Commonwealth of Virginia Home Page:
www.virginia.gov

The Official Tourism Website of the Commonwealth of Virginia:
www.virginia.org

ABOUT THE AUTHOR

David C. King is an award-winning author who has written more than forty books for children and young adults.

Laura L. Sullivan is the author of many books for children, including the novels Under the Green Hill, Guardian of the Green Hill, Ladies in Waiting, and Love by the Morning Star.

Stephanie Fitzgerald has been writing nonfiction for children for more than ten years, and she is the author of more than twenty books.

Index

Page numbers in **boldface** are illustrations.

Index